Anne Frank

JUNIOR ■ WORLD ■ BIOGRAPHIES

Anne Frank

SANDOR KATZ

CHELSEA JUNIORS

a division of CHELSEA HOUSE PUBLISHERS

English-language words that are italicized in the text can be found in the glossary at the back of the book.

Chelsea House Publishers

EDITORIAL DIRECTOR Richard Rennert
EXECUTIVE MANAGING EDITOR Karyn Gullen Browne
COPY CHIEF Robin James
PICTURE EDITOR Adrian G. Allen
CREATIVE DIRECTOR Robert Mitchell
ART DIRECTOR Joan Ferrigno
PRODUCTION MANAGER Sallye Scott

JUNIOR WORLD BIOGRAPHIES

SENIOR EDITOR Martin Schwabacher
SERIES DESIGN Marjorie Zaum

Staff for ANNE FRANK

EDITORIAL ASSISTANTS Scott D. Briggs, Erin McKenna
PICTURE RESEARCHER Sandy Jones
COVER DESIGN Marjorie Zaum

5 7 9 8 6 4

Library of Congress Cataloging-in-Publication Data
Katz, Sandor
  Anne Frank / Sandor Katz.
    p. cm.—(Junior world biographies)
  Includes bibliographical references and index.
Summary: Traces the life of the young Jewish girl whose
diary chronicles the years she and her family hid from the Nazis
in an Amsterdam attic.
ISBN 0-7910-2120-3
      0-7910-2121-1 (pbk.)
  1. Frank, Anne, 1929–1945—Juvenile literature. 2. Holocaust,
Jewish(1939–1945)—Netherlands—Amsterdam—Biography—
Juvenile literature. 3. Jews—Netherlands—Amsterdam—
Biography—Juvenile literature. 4. Amsterdam(Netherlands)—
Biography—Juvenile literature. [1. Frank, Anne, 1929–   .
2. Jews—Biography. 3. Holocaust, Jewish (1939–1945)—Nether-
lands—Amsterdam.] I. Title. II. Series.
DS135.N6F7337 1996
940.53'18'092—dc20   95-22175
[B]   CIP
                                                            AC

Contents

On October 10, 1942, Anne pasted this
picture in her diary with the note, "This is a
photo as I would wish myself to look all
the time. Then I would maybe have a chance to
come to Hollywood."

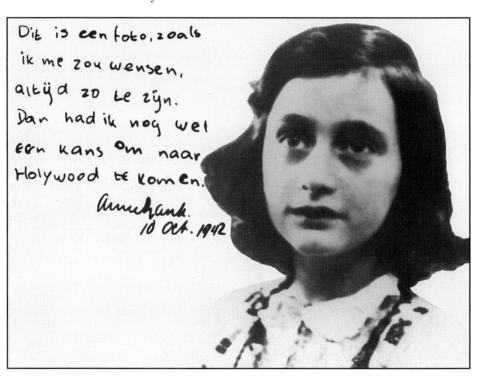

1

"Where Would We Go?"

Anne Frank woke up early on the morning of June 12, 1942. She was very excited because it was her 13th birthday. She waited until seven o'clock, then woke up her parents so she could open her birthday presents.

Anne received many presents from her parents and her friends. Her gifts included a party game, a jigsaw puzzle, jewelry, candy, flowers, lots of books, and some money. Anne's favorite birthday present, however, was the first one she opened—a diary. Anne had many friends but none she felt could really understand her innermost secrets. "I want this diary itself to be my friend," she wrote, "and I shall call my friend Kitty."

Anne started writing in her diary two days later. She wrote about her life and about her family and friends. Anne told funny stories, such as the time her math teacher made her write a composition called "A Chatterbox" because she talked too much in class. She wrote about feeling lonely and described her most private feelings, what she called "things that lie buried deep in my heart." And she also wrote about the dramatic political events going on around her during World War II.

Anne had great ambitions to become a journalist, and she loved to write. "I can shake off everything if I write," Anne wrote in her diary; "my sorrows disappear, my courage is reborn. But . . . will I ever be able to write anything great, will I ever become a journalist or a writer?" As she began keeping her diary, Anne could not have imagined that one day millions of people all over the world would read it.

Anne and her family were Jewish. They came from a religious background that was different from most people around them. The Jewish religion started long before Christianity. Over and over again throughout history, Jewish people as a group have been unfairly blamed for all sorts of problems. Long ago the Catholic church hunted and killed Jews, along with others who chose to follow different religions. This was called the Inquisition. In many places and many times, Jews have been outcasts.

Jewish people are a minority group in Europe and the United States. Often people who are part of any minority group face *prejudice*—individuals being judged unfairly simply for being part of a particular group. Prejudice against minorities often results in unfair treatment or discrimination. Anne and her family faced a form of prejudice and discrimination known as *anti-Semitism,* the hatred of Jewish or Arab people.

The Frank family lived in the Netherlands, which is also known as Holland. In May 1940, during the early part of World War II, the Netherlands was invaded by the Nazi army. The Nazis had first come to power in Germany. Now they were taking over the Netherlands, too. The Nazis were trying to kill all the Jews and other minority groups they did not like, such as Gypsies, homosexuals, and communists.

German chancellor and Nazi leader Adolf Hitler greets thousands of Hitler Youth at a stadium in 1935. The Nazis encouraged Germans to hate Jews, homosexuals, people of color, and others they labeled inferior.

Early in July 1942, about three weeks after her birthday, Anne was out walking with her father, Otto Frank. They were in Amsterdam, the biggest city in the Netherlands, where they lived. Mr. Frank had been forced by the Nazis to leave the spice business he had started, simply because he was Jewish. As he walked with Anne that summer day, he told her of his plans for the family to go into hiding.

Mr. Frank had been preparing a hiding place for many months. He had stored a great deal of food, supplies, and furniture in the hiding place. Mr. Frank had also asked several of the people who used to work for him to help take care of him and his family.

"We shall disappear of our own accord," he explained to Anne, "and not wait until they come and fetch us." But he did not tell Anne where they would be hiding or any other details. "Don't worry about it," he told her. "We shall arrange everything. Make the most of your carefree young life while you can."

Hearing this news, Anne was no longer so carefree. "Where would we go?" she wondered in her diary. "In a town or the country? In a house or a cottage? When, how, where . . . ?" She did not have to wait long to find out.

At three o'clock in the afternoon that Sunday, the doorbell rang at the Frank home. Anne's friend Harry Goldberg had been over earlier in the day. Anne was expecting Harry back later in the afternoon. In the meantime, she was enjoying the summer sunshine, reading a book on the back porch.

Suddenly, Anne's older sister Margot appeared in the kitchen doorway. Margot looked very upset. She told Anne that the Nazis had just been at the front door. "Mummy has gone to the Van Daans to discuss whether we should move into our hiding place tomorrow," reported Margot. "The Van Daans are going with us." Hermann Van Daan had worked in the spice business with Mr. Frank. He and his wife Petronella and their 15-year-old son, Peter, were also Jewish. "So we shall be seven in all," Margot said.

Anne's mother, Edith Frank, returned to the house with the Van Daans. While the adults were discussing plans, Anne and Margot were sent upstairs to their room. While they were alone together, Anne learned that the Nazis had come looking for Margot. "I was more frightened than ever and began to cry," wrote Anne. "Margot is sixteen; would they really take girls of that age away alone?" Now she really understood the importance of hiding from the Nazis.

The doorbell rang again. Anne thought it must be Harry, so she started to go answer the door. Margot held her back. Anne could not open the door because nobody, not even their friends, could know they were going into hiding. Anne heard her mother send Harry away. She never saw Harry again.

Anne began to pack her bags, still unsure where she would be going or for how long. "The first thing I put in was this diary, then hair curlers, handkerchiefs, schoolbooks, a comb, old letters; I put in the craziest things. . . . But I'm not sorry, memories mean more to me than dresses."

Meanwhile, Mr. Van Daan went to notify the Dutch friends who would be helping them. It would be impossible to hide without help from the outside. They needed people to bring them food and news—and simply to keep their spirits up. But helping Jews to hide was a dangerous thing to do. If Dutch people were caught helping Jews, they could be arrested and even killed.

"The Franks have decided to go immediately into hiding," Mr. Van Daan whispered to Miep Gies and her husband, Jan. "Can you come right now and take a few things that they'll need in hiding?" Miep and Jan made two trips carrying the Franks' clothing to their house. They planned to bring the clothes to the hiding place after the Franks were there.

After a busy and anxious night, the Franks were ready to leave their home and go into hiding early the next morning. The date was Monday, July 6, 1942. "We put on heaps of clothes as if we were going to the North Pole, the sole reason being to take clothes with us," wrote Anne. "No Jew in our situation would have dreamed of going out with a suitcase full of clothing. I had on two vests, three pairs of pants, a dress, on top of that a skirt, jacket, summer coat, two pairs of stockings, lace-up shoes, woolly cap, scarf, and still more."

At 7:30 A.M., Anne said good-bye to her cat Moortje and left her comfortable home. She and her parents walked out of their house into the morning rain. Only after they were walking through the streets of Amsterdam did Mr. and Mrs. Frank tell Anne where they were going. The hiding place turned out to be some hidden rooms in the upstairs of the building where Mr. Frank's spice business was located, at Prinsengracht 263. Anne called it the Secret Annex in her diary.

German soldiers watch as the Dutch city of Rotterdam goes up in flames in May 1940. The Nazis forced the Netherlands to surrender in just four days.

2

"The Good Times Rapidly Fled"

In her diary, Anne carefully described her life in hiding. She and her family and the Van Daan family were confined to a small space, much smaller than a school classroom. They could not leave this small space. "I can't tell you how oppressive it is never to be able to go outdoors," wrote Anne. "Also I'm very afraid that we shall be discovered and shot."

Anne could not see her friends or go to school. The only outside contact Anne and the others had was with the five Dutch non-Jewish people who helped them hide and brought them food. One of these brave friends was Miep Gies. Whenever Miep visited, Anne was full of questions. "Have you seen my cat, Moortje?" she would ask. "What about my friends?" Miep remembers that Anne was always "longing for news."

Miep and three of the other helpers worked together running the spice business that Mr. Frank had started and was forced to give up by the Nazis. The business was located downstairs from the Secret Annex. The other three helpers in the office were named Jo Koophuis, Victor Kraler, and Elli Vossen. The fifth helper was Miep's husband, Jan Gies, who visited almost every day. Anne called them "the soup eaters" in her diary because often when they visited they would stay for a cup of soup. These five brave people risked their lives by helping Anne and the others.

This was not the first time the Franks had been forced to escape from the Nazis. Although

Anne had spent most of her life in the Netherlands, she was not originally from Holland. Anne was born in Frankfurt, Germany, on June 12, 1929. Her father's family had lived in that city for hundreds of years. The family was in the banking business and had a comfortable and stable life there. Frankfurt had a large Jewish community, and Jews had been accepted as part of the city.

During Anne's early childhood years, the Nazi party became very powerful in Germany. The Nazis blamed all of Germany's problems on the Jews. They claimed that Germans were the "mas-

The young Anne Frank is admired by her mother and her sister, Margot. Anne was just one month old when her father took this picture in 1929.

ter race," and that Jews were inferior. The Nazis passed many laws against Jewish people. For instance, Jews were not allowed to work at certain jobs, and Jewish children could only attend Jewish schools.

The leader of the Nazi party, Adolf Hitler, became the ruler of Germany in March 1933, when Anne was not yet four years old. Many Jews left Germany to escape the Nazis. Anne's grandmother went to Switzerland. Some of her relatives came to the United States. The Frank family moved to Holland, where Jews could live freely. The Netherlands had a tradition of respect for people of different beliefs. Jews were accepted as human beings there, as they had been in earlier times in Germany.

The move to Holland was a big change for Anne. She had to leave her home, her friends, her school, and all that she had known. The Netherlands has its own language, Dutch, so at first Anne could not even understand people talking in her new country.

Anne learned Dutch quickly, made new friends, and did well in school. The Frank family was happy with its new home in Holland. The Nazis, however, were not satisfied with ruling Germany. They were intent on gaining control over all of Europe. In 1937, they took over Austria, and in 1939, they attacked Poland, causing war to break out throughout Europe. On May 10, 1940, the Nazi army invaded Holland.

Germany is much bigger than Holland and has many more people, and its army was much stronger than Holland's. Within four days of the attack, the Nazis had taken over the Netherlands. The Dutch Queen, Wilhelmina, escaped to Britain. She was able to speak to the Dutch people on the radio, but the Nazis had taken over the government and ran the country. As Anne described it in her diary, "the good times rapidly fled."

For the Franks and other Jews, the Nazi takeover meant they would have to live with hateful anti-Jewish laws. As Anne wrote in her diary, "Jews must wear a yellow star, Jews must hand in their bicycles, Jews are banned from trains and forbidden to drive. Jews are only allowed to do their shopping between three and five o'clock and then only in shops which bear the placard 'Jewish shop.' Jews must be indoors by eight o'clock and cannot even sit in their own gardens after that hour. Jews are forbidden to visit theaters, cinemas,

In countries controlled by the Nazis, Jewish people had to wear yellow stars in public as part of a government-sponsored system of discrimination.

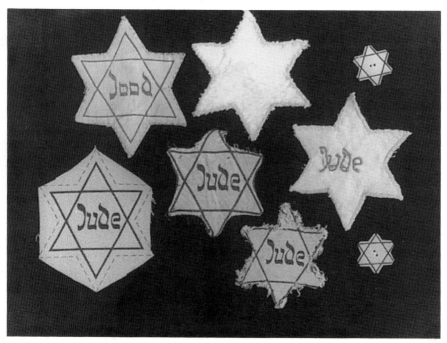

and other places of entertainment. Jews may not take part in public sports. Swimming baths, tennis courts, hockey fields, and other sports grounds are all prohibited to them. Jews may not visit Christians. Jews must go to Jewish schools, and many more restrictions of a similar kind."

Jews were not the only people whose lives were touched by the Nazis. The Nazis discriminated against other minorities, too. They sent many Dutch people to work camps in Germany to keep the Nazi army well supplied. All Dutch students were forced to pledge their support to the Nazis and what the Nazis called "the New Order." Anne reported in her diary that most of the Dutch students refused to go against their consciences. "Naturally they had to bear the consequences," wrote Anne. This meant being sent to German work camps. "What will be left of the youth of this country," asked Anne, "if they have all got to do hard labor in Germany?"

Even worse than labor camps were concentration camps, where Jews were being taken by the

Nazis. The concentration camps were worse than anything imaginable. People were taken from their homes and crowded into railroad cars and trucks that took them to these camps, like cattle being sent to slaughter. "Families are torn apart," wrote Anne, "the men, women, and children all being separated. Children coming home from school find that their parents have disappeared. Women return from shopping to find their homes shut up and their families gone." Sometimes, the Nazi guards would shoot someone on the spot because they cried out to be reunited with their children. Other people were shot for no reason at all.

At the camps, everybody was a prisoner. They were forced to work very hard. If they did not work fast enough, they could be shot. People were fed hardly anything. Photographs from the camps show people who look as if they are little more than skin and bones, starving and near death. The camps were crowded and dirty, and many prisoners caught deadly diseases.

Worst of all, some of the camps were "death camps." Prisoners, including young children, were marched into gas chambers. After they were trapped in these rooms, poisonous gas would be sprayed in. Within minutes, everyone in the room would be dead. Their bodies were cleared out and burned in huge ovens to make room for the next group to be brutally murdered. The Nazis killed huge numbers of people in these concentration camps, including about six million Jews.

Although the Nazis tried to keep the death camps a secret and called them "labor camps," Anne and her family knew what the Nazis were doing. "We assume that most of them are murdered," wrote Anne. "As for us, we are fortunate. Yes, we are luckier than millions of people." But even with a place to hide, the Franks were scared that they would be found and taken away by the Nazis to these horrible camps.

Anne's family hid from the Nazis in this
building located behind her father's warehouse.
During her years in hiding, Anne spent many
hours peeking through the attic window at
the world outside.

3

Adjusting to Life in the Secret Annex

Living in the Secret Annex was like an endless, life-or-death game of hide-and-seek. Being seen or heard would mean that Anne and the others would be caught, sent to concentration camps, and probably killed.

The Secret Annex was upstairs from the office of Mr. Frank's spice and pectin business and behind a storage warehouse. It was separated from the warehouse by a door. This door was hidden behind a movable bookcase built by one of their helpers.

The Secret Annex consisted of two floors. The Franks lived downstairs. Anne and Margot shared one room, their parents another. The Van Daans, who moved in a week after the Franks, slept upstairs, where the kitchen was. There was also an attic space above the front of the office.

When they first moved in, Anne and her father worked hard to clean the Secret Annex and make it comfortable to live in. "Our room looked very bare at first with nothing on the walls," wrote Anne. "But thanks to Daddy who had brought my film-star collection and picture postcards on beforehand . . . I have transformed the walls into one gigantic picture."

Everyone in the Secret Annex had to move carefully so they would not be seen or heard. During working hours, they had to be silent so the workers beneath them would not hear them. This meant Anne and the others had to spend their days upstairs. All day long they had to whisper and move around on tiptoe. During the day, they could not use the toilet because it was downstairs. In the evening they could move around more freely. But at night they had to make sure all the windows were well covered so they could not be seen by neighbors. One wrong move might give them all away.

The Franks and the Van Daans could not leave any clues of their presence in the Secret Annex. For example, even in warm weather they had to make fires to burn vegetable peelings and trash. "We can't put anything into the garbage pails," wrote Anne, "because we must always think of the warehouse boy."

Living in such a small space with so many people was not easy. "Why do grown-ups quarrel so easily, so much, and over the most idiotic things?" Anne asked Kitty. She wrote, "Up till now I thought that only children squabbled and that that wore off as you grew up." Anne felt that everyone was always telling her what to do. "Nothing, I repeat, nothing about me is right; my general appearance, my character, my manners are discussed from A to Z."

Anne was very close to her father but frequently quarreled with her mother and her sister. Once the Van Daans moved in, Anne had difficulties with them as well. She felt that Mrs. Van Daan was always bossing her around. "These are always her first and last words 'if Anne were my daughter.' Thank heavens I'm not!" Anne and Mr. Van Daan "usually manage to upset each other," she wrote. As for Peter, "he is so boring; he flops lazily on his bed half the time, does a bit of carpentry, and then goes back for another snooze. What a fool."

Mr. and Mrs. Van Daan often fought with each other as well. "The yells and screams, stamping and abuse—you can't possibly imagine it!" reported Anne. "My family stood at the bottom of the stairs, holding their breath, ready if necessary to drag them apart." All this fighting made everyone nervous. Anne found peace and quiet only in her diary.

Life in the Secret Annex was difficult, but it was much better than a concentration camp. Anne wrote, "I feel wicked sleeping in a warm bed, while my dearest friends have been knocked down or have fallen into a gutter somewhere out in the cold

Men and women are separated at Auschwitz, a Nazi death camp. After being stripped and tattooed with a number, the prisoners were worked to death or killed in gas chambers.

night. I get frightened when I think of close friends who have now been delivered into the hands of the cruelest brutes that walk the earth. And all because they are Jews!"

When the Franks and Van Daans had a chance to help another Jew, they did. Even though it was very hard living together in such a small space, they decided to invite an eighth person to hide with them in the Secret Annex. A Jewish friend of the Frank family, Albert Dussel, was a dentist. Miep continued going to see him, even though the Nazis had made it illegal for non-Jewish people to use the services of Jews. One day while Miep was visiting his office, Dr. Dussel whispered to her, "Miep, perhaps you know of a hiding place for me?"

Miep had an idea. She thought maybe Dr. Dussel could join the others already hiding in the Secret Annex. But Miep could not tell Dr. Dussel that she knew of a possible hiding place, because she could not tell anyone about the Secret Annex.

As soon as Miep got back to her office, she went u Frank about Dr. Dussel's question. The Franks and Van Daans discussed it. A few days later, Mr. Frank said to Miep, "Where seven can eat, eight people can eat as well." Miep made all the arrangements, and Dr. Dussel moved into the Secret Annex soon after.

Margot moved into Mr. and Mrs. Frank's room, and Dr. Dussel moved into Anne's room. "Quite honestly I'm not so keen that a stranger should use my things," wrote Anne. "But one must be prepared to make some sacrifices for a good cause, so I shall make my little offering with good will. 'If we can save someone, then everything else is of secondary importance,' says Daddy, and he's absolutely right."

Anne was extremely grateful to Miep and the other people who had saved their lives. Anne wrote in her diary:

Never have we heard one word of the bur-
den which we certainly must be to them,

never has one of them complained of all the trouble we give. They all come upstairs every day, talk to the men about business and politics, to the women about food and wartime difficulties, and about newspapers and books with the children. They put on the brightest possible faces, bring flowers and presents for birthdays and bank holidays, are always ready to help and do all they can. That is something we must never forget; although others may show heroism in the war or against the Germans, our helpers display heroism in their cheerfulness and affection.

Providing for eight people in hiding was a lot of work. "Miep is just like a pack mule," Anne told Kitty. "She fetches and carries so much. Almost every day she manages to get hold of some vegetables for us and brings everything in shopping bags on her bicycle."

It was often very difficult for Miep to find food to bring. Because of the war there were food shortages. These got worse as the war went on. Miep remembers, "It was not unusual to wait in a long line at a shop, finally get to the counter, and find that there was almost nothing to buy: a few beans, some wilted lettuce, half-rotted potatoes. But never did I hear a complaint from the hiding place."

Anne and the others made the best of their situation. They found ways to amuse themselves. Sometimes they were silly, such as when Anne and Peter Van Daan dressed up. One night, wrote Anne, "He appeared in one of Mrs. Van Daan's very narrow dresses and I put on his suit. . . . The grownups were doubled over with laughter and we enjoyed ourselves as much as they did."

Anne had many hobbies that helped to pass the time. The most important one to her was writing. She also loved family trees—especially of the European royal families—and reading about history. "I can hardly wait for the day that I shall be able to comb through the books in a public library," she wrote. Anne was also interested in Greek and Roman myths, as well as film stars and family photos. Books from the outside were as important to her as food. "We always long for Saturdays when our books come," she wrote. "Just like little children receiving a present. Ordinary people simply don't know what books mean to us, shut up here. Reading, learning and the radio are our amusements."

One night the residents of the Secret Annex had a slumber party with Miep and her husband. This was a special treat for Anne and the others in hiding because it was different from the same old routine. For Miep, it was very scary. "I became aware of what it meant to be imprisoned in these small rooms," she remembers. "I felt a taste of the helpless fear that these people were filled with, day and night. . . . For the first time I knew what it was like to be a Jew in hiding."

For Anne, the danger of her situation weighed on her daily. Her life before moving to the Secret Annex began to seem unreal. "If I think back to our old house, my girl friends, the fun at school, it is just as if another person lived it all, not me," she wrote. But she never lost her hope that one day she would have her life back. As she wrote after a year and a half in hiding:

> *The sun is shining, the sky is a deep blue, there is a lovely breeze and I'm longing—so longing—for everything. To talk, for freedom, for friends, to be alone. And I do so long . . . to cry! I feel as if I'm going to burst, and I know that it would get better with crying; but I can't, I'm restless, I go from one room to the other, breathe through the crack of a closed window, feel my heart beating, as if it is saying, 'Can't you satisfy my longings at last?'*

U.S. general Dwight D. Eisenhower speaks to Allied troops in England just before a major counterattack against the Nazis. During their time in hiding, the Franks listened closely to news of the war on the radio.

4

Terrors and Hopes in the Secret Annex

Anne sometimes wondered if the living nightmare of being trapped in the Secret Annex would ever end. "Believe me," she wrote in December 1943, "if you have been shut up for a year and a half, it can get too much for you some days. . . . I am simply a young girl badly in need of some rollicking fun!" A month later, she wrote, "If I stay here for very long I shall grow into a dried-up old beanstalk. And I did so want to grow into a real young woman!"

Anne and the others listened to the news reports on the radio every day for signs of hope. "As the news from outside gets worse," wrote Anne, "so the radio with its miraculous voice helps us to keep up our morale and to say again, 'Chins up, stick it out, better times will come!'" They would cheer as they listened to speeches by U.S. general Dwight Eisenhower, British prime minister Winston Churchill, and Queen Wilhelmina of the Netherlands, who spoke from exile in Britain.

The Allied forces, which included the United States, Britain, and the Soviet Union, were at war with Nazi Germany. The only hope that Anne and the others had for freedom was the defeat of the Nazis. "Sometime this war will be over," wrote Anne. "Surely the time will come when we are people again, and not just Jews."

Each report of hopeful news brought with it dreams of life out of hiding. "Perhaps, Margot says, I may yet be able to go back to school in September," wrote Anne in June 1944, after nearly two years in hiding. Miep remembers one visit to the hiding place, when "Anne began to try on her clothes, imagining what she could wear back to school."

But along with times of hope came times of fear. One of the scariest times for Anne was April 9, 1944, the night the warehouse connected to the Secret Annex was robbed. That night, a noise was heard from beneath the Secret Annex. Mr. Frank, Mr. Van Daan, Dr. Dussel, and Peter Van Daan went downstairs to investigate. They found burglars trying to break into the office, so they shouted "Police!" to scare the thieves away. This worked and sent the thieves running.

Unfortunately, other people were outside and heard the shouts. Someone shined a flashlight into the office, and the four Jewish men hiding inside feared that they had been seen. When they came back upstairs to the Secret Annex, Mr. Frank was nervous and pale with fright. "Lights out, creep upstairs," he announced. "We expect the police in the house."

For the eight Jews in hiding, the police were much more dangerous than any thieves. As Miep put it, "The times were such that a thief was safe and a Jew was not." The Nazi police would send Anne and the others to concentration camps if they found them. Mr. Frank figured that the people who heard the shouts of "Police" had called the police. After nearly two years of hiding from the Nazis, Anne and the others thought they were about to be discovered. "Think of it, waiting in such fear!" Anne wrote in her diary. "No one had anything to suggest, so we simply sat there in pitch-darkness."

After a while, late that night, they heard the sounds of people entering the building. Was it the Nazi police? Was it the thieves? Anne and the others trembled with fear. They heard footsteps downstairs, then the sound of someone coming up the stairs. Finally, they heard the bookcase that hid the door to the Secret Annex being rattled. "Now we are lost!" said Anne. She pictured the Nazi police behind the door coming to take them away. "This moment is indescribable," she wrote in her diary. Anne had never been so terrified in all her life.

The bookcase rattled once again. "Then there was nothing, the footsteps withdrew, we

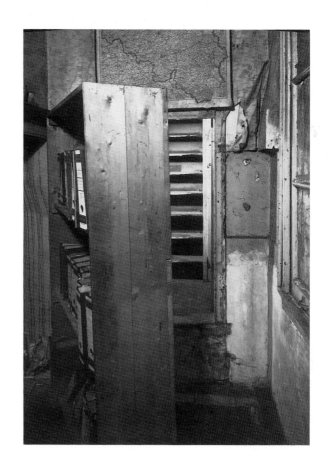

The staircase leading to the Secret Annex was hidden behind this swinging bookcase.

were saved so far." But the police, or whoever the intruders were, had left a candle burning near the bookcase. "Perhaps the police had forgotten the light?" they wondered. "Would someone come back to put it out? Perhaps there was someone on guard outside?" They still did not dare to move. They used a tin garbage can as a toilet. Anne thought it smelled terrible.

As they thought about the possibility of being caught, they talked about destroying some of their things. For instance, the radio they listened to was illegal for Jews to have. And they thought that Anne's diary might contain information that could be used against them and their helpers. "Not my diary!" Anne protested. "If my diary goes, I go with it." They let Anne keep her diary. The next day their helpers were back and life returned to normal, or as normal as it could be in hiding.

That night of terror changed Anne's life. "During that night I really felt that I had to die, I waited for the police, I was prepared, as the soldier is on the battlefield," she wrote in her diary. But once the crisis had passed, Anne dreamed of the life ahead of her. Anne viewed herself as "a woman with inward strength and plenty of courage." She promised herself, "I shall not remain insignificant, I shall work in the world and for mankind!"

It took much strength and courage to survive in hiding. A war was going on around the Secret Annex. In addition to thieves and police, Anne and the others lived in fear of gunfire and bombs from the air. They could be killed by a bomb, or if their building was damaged or caught fire, their hiding place would be lost.

Air raid warnings were common. Sometimes bombs fell nearby. "The house rumbled and shook," wrote Anne after one air raid, "and down came the bombs." Some nights Anne spent wide awake with fear, listening. "We don't have a single quiet night," she complained to Kitty. "I creep into Daddy's bed nearly every night for comfort," she wrote. During one night of exploding bombs, "I clasped my 'escape bag' close to me, more because I wanted something to hold than with the idea of escaping, because there's nowhere we can go."

Anne's life in hiding was filled with smaller challenges as well. When they first came to live in the Secret Annex in 1942, Anne was 13 years old. After two years in hiding, she was 15. Miep described her as "little Anne, who was turning into not-so-little Anne before our very eyes. She was simply bursting out of her clothes, and her body was changing shape as well. . . . Nature was moving her right along, despite the conditions forced upon her."

Wartime shortages made clothes hard to find. Miep and the other helpers brought second-hand clothes to the Secret Annex. Mostly they brought simple, practical things. But Miep decided to look for something "grown-up and pretty" for Anne. One day, Miep found the perfect treat: a pair of red high-heeled shoes. "Never have I seen anyone so happy as Anne was that day," she remembers.

Anne wrote in her diary about the changes she was going through during puberty. "I think what is happening to me is so wonderful," she wrote, "and not only what can be seen on my body, but all that is taking place inside." When she began to menstruate, she called it "my sweet secret." Confined to the Secret Annex, Anne had no friends to share these secrets with. "If only I had a girlfriend!" she wrote.

As Anne grew older, she became closer to Peter Van Daan. Anne shared many secrets with Peter. They spent many hours sitting together and talking in the attic of the Secret Annex. They talked about their problems and their parents and their lives before going into hiding. They even talked about sex. Anne wrote, "There really are young people—and of the opposite sex too—who can discuss these things naturally without making fun of them." As they grew closer, Anne confided to her diary that "From early in the morning till late at night, I really do hardly anything else but think of Peter."

When she first met Peter Van Daan, Anne thought he was very dull, but as she grew older and began spending more time with him, the two became very close.

Anne marked Saturday, April 15, 1944, as a special day in her diary because it was the day she and Peter first kissed. She had kissed girlfriends before, but this was the first time with a boy. She asked Kitty, "Do you think that Daddy and Mummy would approve of my sitting and kissing a boy?" After she talked to her father, she wrote

"Daddy doesn't want me to go upstairs so much in the evenings now." But Anne had an independent spirit and liked to make decisions for herself, and she resolved, "I'm going."

Her romance with Peter brought new hope and appreciation to Anne's difficult life in hiding. "Is there anything more beautiful in the world," she asked Kitty a few days later, "than to sit before an open window and enjoy nature, to listen to the birds singing, feel the sun on your cheeks and have a darling boy in your arms?"

Even after two years in hiding, Anne felt hopeful about the future. "I regard our hiding as a dangerous adventure, romantic and interesting at the same time," she wrote in the spring of 1944. She felt that her experience in hiding had strengthened her, and she had big ambitions to become a famous writer. Unlike her mother, who was a housewife, "I must have something besides a husband and children, something that I can devote myself to!" wrote Anne. "I want to go on living even after my death!"

In 1987, Miep Gies revealed her true identity and published a book, Anne Frank Remembered: The Story of the Woman Who Helped To Hide the Frank Family. *She is shown here with her husband, Jan, by the entrance to the Secret Annex.*

5

The Police Come

Anne longed for contact with nature. "I wonder if it's because I haven't been able to poke my nose outdoors for so long that I've grown so crazy about everything to do with nature?" she asked Kitty. One night, Anne went to the attic and found the window open. It was dark and rainy outside. The wind was strong. "It was the first time in a year and a half that I'd seen the night face to face. After that evening my longing to see it again was greater than my fear of burglars, rats, and raids on the house. . . . To look up at the sky, the clouds, the moon, and the stars makes me calm and patient. . . . Mother Nature makes me humble and prepared to face every blow courageously."

Life grew harder in the Secret Annex the longer they were there. Anne wrote, "I feel afraid sometimes that from having to be so serious I'll grow a long face and my mouth will droop at the corners." The bombing in Amsterdam grew worse. Food became scarcer than ever. "I simply can't imagine that the world will ever be normal for us again," wrote Anne. "I do talk about 'after the war,' but then it is only a castle in the air, something that will never really happen."

The eight Jews in hiding were tired of being cooped up together in the same cramped space. On Friday, June 16, 1944, Anne reported "New problems: Mrs. Van Daan is desperate, talks about a bullet through her head, prison, hanging, suicide." Everyone was nervous and jumpy. Anne felt criticized by all the others and was forced inside herself to look for "a way of becoming what I would so like to be, and what I could be, if . . . there weren't any other people living in the world."

These were the last words Anne Frank wrote in her diary. She wrote them on Tuesday, August 1, 1944.

Three days later, on Friday, August 4, 1944, the Nazi police came to the Secret Annex and arrested Anne and the seven other Jews in hiding. To this day, nobody has figured out how the police discovered their hiding place. Whoever reported them to the police received the standard Nazi reward of $1.40 per Jew, for a total of $11.20. Jewish lives were cheap under the Nazis. Victor Kraler and Jo Koophuis, two of their helpers, were arrested with them. They were sent to prison, and the Jews were taken to concentration camps.

Miep and Jan were not arrested. After the arrests Miep went upstairs to the Secret Annex. "On the floor, amidst the chaos of papers and books, my eye lit on the little red-orange checkered, cloth-bound diary that Anne had received from her father on her thirteenth birthday." Miep gathered Anne's diary and other writings. Without reading them, she stored Anne's writings in the bottom drawer of her desk. "I'll keep everything safe for Anne until she comes back," she said. When people in the office asked to read them, Miep would not let them. "It's hers and it's her secret. I'll only return it back into her hands and her hands alone."

Less than a month after Anne's arrest, on September 3, 1944, British troops entered the Netherlands. The Dutch people were hopeful that soon they would be free of the Nazis. Jo Koophuis returned to Amsterdam, after the prison camp he was detained in was liberated by British troops. This gave Miep and the others hope that Anne and the other Jews would soon be free. On April 30, 1945, Hitler killed himself, and a week later, on May 7, Germany surrendered. The war was over. "To wake up and go through a whole day without

In October 1944, Anne and Margot were sent to this camp, Bergen-Belsen. Their parents remained in Auschwitz, where Anne's mother died in January 1945.

any sense of danger was amazing," remembers Miep. "And right away, Jan and I and everyone else began waiting to see just who would be coming home to us."

On June 3, Otto Frank returned to Amsterdam and came to stay with Miep and Jan. Mr. Frank had been at a concentration camp in Poland called Auschwitz. He knew that Anne and Margot and their mother had been taken to Auschwitz with him. But at Auschwitz he had been separated from them.

After the camp was freed, Mr. Frank learned that his wife, Edith, had died at Auschwitz. He also discovered that Anne and Margot, along with Mrs. Van Daan, had been transferred to a camp in Germany called Bergen-Belsen. At Auschwitz, Mr. Frank had seen Mr. Van Daan on his way to the gas chambers to be killed. He did not know what had happened to the others. Every day, Mr. Frank searched for news of Anne and Margot.

One morning, about two months after Mr. Frank's return to Amsterdam, a letter arrived with news. After a long silence, Mr. Frank told Miep, "Margot and Anne are not coming back." The Bergen-Belsen camp was dirty and crowded and full of disease. First Margot had gotten sick with typhus, a terrible disease accompanied by very high fevers, and died in late February or early March. Then Anne, all alone, had gotten the same disease and died just weeks before World War II ended.

A childhood friend of Anne's, Lies Goosens, had seen Anne at the Bergen-Belsen camp. Lies was taken to the camp earlier in the war, while Anne was living in the Secret Annex. At one point, when she was still safely in hiding, Anne had a dream about Lies. "Oh, Anne," asked Lies in the dream, "why have you deserted me? Help, oh, help me, rescue me from this hell!" When they met at the concentration camp, "It wasn't the same Anne," Lies later said. "She was a broken girl. I probably was, too, but it was so terrible. She immediately began to cry, and she told me, 'I don't have parents anymore.'. . . I always think if Anne had known that her father was still alive, she might have had more strength to survive."

A woman suffering from starvation and overwork lies in her bunk in Bergen-Belsen. Anne and Margot Frank both died at this camp in 1945, less than two months before it was liberated by the British.

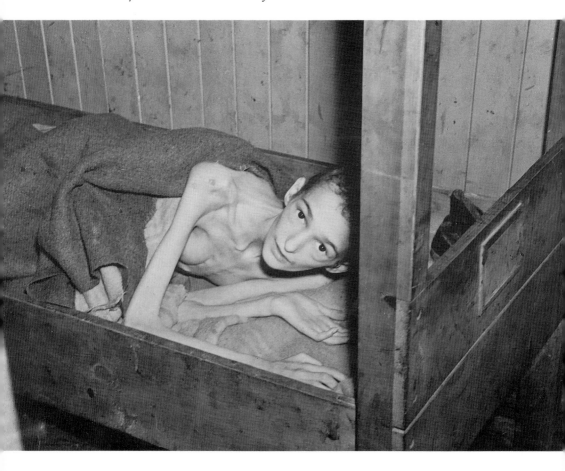

When news of Anne's death arrived, Miep gathered the diary and other papers she had been saving for Anne's return. She carried them into Mr. Frank's office and said, "Here is your daughter Anne's legacy to you." The diaries became Anne's legacy not only to her father but to the world.

*Anne Frank's father speaks with schoolchildren
at the Anne Frank School in Düsseldorf, Germany,
in 1959.*

6

Anne Frank's Legacy

Otto Frank wanted to share Anne's powerful writings. He selected the parts he thought were most important and had them typed and copied for his friends to read. One of his friends gave a copy of the diary to a respected Dutch historian, who wrote an article about it that appeared in a Dutch newspaper in 1946. A year later, the diary was published in the Netherlands as *Het Achterhuis,* Dutch for "The Secret Annex."

Anne's diary was published in English in 1952. In English, it is known as *Anne Frank: The Diary of a Young Girl*. The diary contains an introduction by Eleanor Roosevelt, the wife of President Franklin Roosevelt, who led the United States during World War II. "This is a remarkable book," wrote Mrs. Roosevelt. "Written by a young girl—and the young are not afraid of telling the truth—it is one of the wisest and most moving commentaries on war and its impact on human beings that I have ever read."

Anne's diary has been translated into more than 55 languages. Over 20 million copies have been printed. Another book of Anne's writings, including short stories, has been published as *Tales from the Secret Annex*. Since her death, Anne Frank has become one of the best-selling authors in the world. Her dream of being a famous writer came true.

Anne's story has also been presented on theater stages as a play. It has been performed in many countries, including Germany, where the

Nazis first came to power. In Germany, the play showed people the impact that their prejudice had on the lives of Jewish people. According to one theater critic, "People did not even go out during intermission. They sat in their seats as if afraid of the light outside, shamed to face each other."

Anne's story has also been made into a movie. In addition, Anne's memory is kept alive by a museum in Amsterdam. The Secret Annex itself, at Prinsengracht 263, has been turned into a museum. Visitors to Amsterdam can actually go inside the space where Anne and the others hid from the Nazis for two years.

Anne's story is just one of millions that ended tragically. Otto Frank was a rare survivor. All of his family and almost all of his Jewish friends were killed in what is known as the Nazi Holocaust. Six million Jews were killed by the Nazis, as well as millions of Gypsies, homosexuals, communists, Catholics, and other innocent people.

In their struggle for survival, the Frank family needed help, which they received from Miep and Jan Gies, Jo Koophuis, Victor Kraler, and Elli Vossen. These brave people risked their own lives to help Anne and the others. They saw how terrible the Nazis were. They decided to do the right thing by helping people who were being attacked by the Nazis. They knew that they were breaking the law, but they knew that the law was unfair.

In her diary, Anne wrote about the many Dutch people who were helping Jews. "It is amazing," she wrote, "how much noble unselfish work these people are doing, risking their own lives to help and save others."

Many of America's greatest heroes are people who have boldly resisted unfair authority. For example, when Harriet Tubman helped runaway slaves escape, it was an act of *resistance*. Tubman knew that even if slavery was legal, it was wrong. So she risked her life to help people break the law, and she helped many slaves escape.

The U.S. civil rights movement is full of examples of resistance. When Rosa Parks refused to give up her seat on a bus to a white person, she was breaking a law. But the law discriminated against African Americans, and it was unfair. Similarly, Nelson Mandela and many others spent years in jail for their actions to end the racist "apartheid" system that discriminated against blacks in South Africa. Their brave acts of resistance helped bring this unjust system to an end, and Mandela went on to become the president of South Africa.

Prejudice and hatred have not gone away. Many minority groups still face discrimination and violence in the United States. Blacks, Arabs, Asians, Latin Americans, lesbians and gay men, people living with AIDS, and Jews often experience terrible prejudice.

Today in Europe, and even in the United States, there are some people who want to return to the policies of the Nazis. These people are called neo-Nazis, meaning new-Nazis. In addition to Jews and homosexuals, they blame foreigners and people of other races for all their problems. Gangs of neo-Nazis have attacked and murdered people, burned down buildings, and destroyed Jewish cemeteries and temples.

Some neo-Nazis claim the Nazi Holocaust never happened. They have even attacked Anne Frank, saying that her diary is a fake. Scientists and historians at the Netherlands State Institute for War Documentation have carefully examined Anne's handwriting, along with the paper, ink, and glue she used, and concluded that the diary is in fact Anne's.

People everywhere have opportunities in their daily lives to carry on Anne Frank's legacy. They can do this by speaking and writing the truth as they see it. "People can tell you to keep your mouth shut," wrote Anne, who was often told to keep quiet by the adults in the Secret Annex. "But it doesn't stop you from having your own opinion. Even if people are still very young, they shouldn't be prevented from saying what they think." Sometimes speaking the truth requires having the courage to resist when authority is used unfairly,

During a ceremony in 1957, a plaque is unveiled at the house where Anne's family lived in Frankfurt, Germany.

whether by parents, school officials, or the government.

After the end of the war, many Germans who served in the Nazi army said that they had only been "following orders." They said they murdered six million Jews because that is what their leaders told them to do. This may be true, but it is a poor excuse. Anne and millions of other European Jews could have been saved if the German people had not blindly followed the Nazi government. Anne's tragic story provides a constant reminder to all citizens of the need to be vigilant and to think for themselves.

Anne's story has a sad ending. She was killed by hate and cruelty. Yet in one of the last entries in her diary, she wrote, "In spite of everything I still believe that people are really good at heart." Anne's voice is as important today as it was when she was living through her horrible nightmare more than fifty years ago. Wars continue to destroy people's lives in many parts of the world. So do prejudice and discrimination.

"What, oh, what is the use of war?" she asked. "Why can't people live peacefully together? Why all this destruction?"

Editor's Note

Because Anne knew that her diary might fall into the hands of the Nazis, she used false names to refer to the people she wrote about. Even after the war, their true identities remained secret for a long time. Today, however, the real names of the people appearing in Anne's diary have been revealed.

Modern editions of Anne's diary still use the names Anne invented, and to avoid confusion, these names were used in this book as well (except for Miep and Jan Gies, whose real names became famous following the publication of Miep's book). The names of the people who lived with Anne in the Secret Annex and their helpers are listed below.

Name given by Anne:	Real Name:
Hermann Van Daan	Hermann van Pels
Petronella Van Daan	Petronella van Pels
Peter Van Daan	Peter van Pels
Albert Dussell	Friedrich Pfeffer
Miep van Santen	Hermine "Miep" Satrouschitz Gies
Henk van Santen	Jan Gies
Jo Koophuis	Johannes Kleiman
Victor Kraler	Victor Gustav Kugler
Elli Vossen	Bep Voskuijl
Lies Goosens	Hannah Elisabeth Pick-Goslar

Further Reading

Amdur, Richard. *Anne Frank*. New York: Chelsea House, 1993.

Frank, Anne. *The Diary of a Young Girl*. New York: Doubleday, 1995.

———. *Tales from the Secret Annex*. New York: Washington Square Press, 1983.

Gies, Miep, with Alison Leslie Gold. *Anne Frank Remembered: The Story of the Woman Who Helped To Hide the Frank Family*. New York: Simon & Schuster, 1987.

van der Rol, Ruud, and Rian Verhoeven, in association with the Anne Frank House. *Anne Frank: Beyond the Diary, A Photographic Remembrance*. New York: Viking, 1993.

Glossary

anti-Semitism   expression of hatred toward people of Jewish or Arab descent

Auschwitz   a death camp in Poland

Bergen-Belsen   a death camp in Germany

communist   a believer in communism, a social system in which the government controls the means of production and all property is owned in common to be used by all as needed

concentration camps   prison camps where Jews and other victims of the Nazis were forced to work extremely hard under starvation conditions and millions were killed in gas chambers

discrimination   unfair judgment and mistreatment of a person based on his or her religious or ethnic background

Inquisition   a court of justice set up by the Roman Catholic church that hunted and killed Jews, along with others who chose to follow different religions

72

master race   the Nazis' image of themselves as a group that was destined to rule the world and that was superior to Jews and other ethnic groups

Nazi Holocaust   the mass killing of six million Jews, as well as millions of Gypsies, homosexuals, communists, Catholics, and other innocent people, by the Nazis.

Nazis   members of the fascist political party of Adolf Hitler, who believed that his government should have total control over his subjects, including the right to silence or kill those who disagreed with him and those who were considered inferior

neo-Nazis   members of a present-day group who support the beliefs and policies of Hitler's Nazis

the New Order   the political movement formed by Hitler to put all of Europe under his rigidly controlled, totalitarian government

prejudice   a belief or opinion formed with little knowledge of the facts

resistance   the act of standing up to unfair authority

Secret Annex   Anne Frank's name for the hiding place of her family, the Van Daans, and Albert Dussel

Chronology

June 12, 1929	Anneliese Marie Frank is born in Frankfurt am Main, Germany
March 1933	Adolf Hitler and the Nazi party take control of Germany
summer 1933	Anne moves with her mother and sister to her grandmother's house in Aachen, Germany, while her father looks for a new home in Amsterdam, the Netherlands
December 5, 1933	Edith and Margot Frank move to Amsterdam
February 1934	Anne Frank joins her family in Amsterdam
September 1, 1939	Germany invades Poland, starting World War II
May 10, 1940	Germany invades and occupies the Netherlands in four days
April 29, 1942	Nazis order all Dutch Jews to wear yellow stars on their clothing

June 12, 1942	On her 13th birthday, Anne gets a diary as a present
July 5, 1942	Margot Frank receives orders to report to the Westerbork work camp
July 6, 1942	The Franks go into hiding in the Secret Annex behind Otto Frank's warehouse
July 13, 1942	The Van Daans join the Franks in their hiding place
November 16, 1942	Albert Dussel moves into the Secret Annex and shares Anne's room
April 9, 1944	Burglars break into the Secret Annex, and the Franks are nearly discovered
June 6, 1944	The Allies launch D day invasion to liberate Europe from the Nazis
August 4, 1944	Anne and the others hiding in the Secret Annex are captured by the police
September 3, 1944	Anne and the others are sent to the Auschwitz death camp in Poland
October 1944	Anne and Margot are transferred to the Bergen-Belsen concentration camp in Germany
January 6, 1945	Edith Frank dies at Auschwitz

January 27, 1945	Otto Frank is freed when the Russians liberate Auschwitz
February 1945	Margot Frank dies at Bergen-Belsen
March 1945	Anne Frank dies of typhus at Bergen-Belsen
May 7, 1945	Germany surrenders, ending the war in Europe
June 1947	Anne's diary is published in Dutch as *Het Achterhuis* (*The Secret Annex*)
1950	*The Secret Annex* is published in Germany and France
1952	Anne's diary is published in English as *Anne Frank: The Diary of a Young Girl*
1955	A play about Anne's life is put on in New York and wins the Pulitzer Prize
August 19, 1980	Otto Frank dies at the age of 91
1987	Miep Gies publishes *Anne Frank Remembered: The Story of the Woman Who Helped To Hide the Frank Family*

Index

Sandor Katz grew up in New York City and attended Brown University, where he graduated with a bachelor's degree in history. He taught at alternative high schools in Providence, Rhode Island, and Chicago, Illinois, before becoming the executive director of a community group in New York City. He then worked as a land-use planner and a Senior Policy Analyst for AIDS for the New York City government. Katz's acts of political resistance include organizing protests against the illegal actions of the U.S. government in Central America and volunteering for the AIDS activists' group ACTUP. His writing has appeared in the *Nation* and *Outweek*.

The author would like to dedicate this book to his comrades living with AIDS and other life-challenging illnesses and to people everywhere struggling for survival in a harsh world. May we all find the courage that Anne Frank did.